# RIB-TICKLERS

**T**o our children,
**Matt, Carrie, and Rebecca, who said,**
**"Quit telling us these corny jokes—**
**write them down instead!"**

The illustrations in this book were done in Dr. Martin's Dyes
The display type was set in Futura Bold Condensed.
The text was set in Goudy Sans. Printed and bound by Tien Wah Press.
Production supervision by Bonnie King. Designed by Teri Sloat.

Inquiries should be addressed to Lothrop, Lee & Shepard Books, a division of
William Morrow & Company, Inc., 1350 Avenue of the Americas, New York, New York 10019.
Printed in Singapore.
First Edition   1 2 3 4 5 6 7 8 9 10
Library of Congress Cataloging in Publication Data
Sloat, Teri.   Rib ticklers : a book of punny animals / by Teri & Robert Sloat.
p.   cm.   ISBN 0-688-12519-0.   1. Animals—Juvenile humor.   2. Puns and punning. [1.
Animals—Wit and humor. 2. Riddles. 3. Jokes.] I. Sloat, Robert. II. Title.   PN6231.A5S58 1994
818'.5402—dc20  93-48619 CIP AC

# TERI & ROBERT SLOAT

# RIB-TICKLERS

# A BOOK OF PUNNY ANIMALS

LOTHROP, LEE & SHEPARD BOOKS    NEW YORK